EXPLORERS WANTED!

On the
South Sea Islands

Simon Chapman

EXPLORERS WANTED!

books by Simon Chapman

Simon Chapman
EXPLORERS
WANTED!

On the South Sea Islands

LITTLE, BROWN AND COMPANY

New York ✤ Boston

Little, Brown and Company

Time Warner Book Group
1271 Avenue of the Americas, New York, NY 10020
Visit our Web site at www.lb-kids.com

First U.S. Edition: September 2005

First published in Great Britain by Egmont Books Limited in 2004

Library of Congress Cataloging-in-Publication Data

On the South Sea Islands/Simon Chapman. — 1st ed.
    p. cm. — (Explorers wanted!)
  ISBN 0-316-15549-7
  1. Natural history — Oceania — Juvenile literature.

  QH198.A106 2005
  919.04 — dc22   2004061550

10 9 8 7 6 5 4 3 2 1

COM-MO

Printed in the United States of America

CONTENTS

SO... YOU WANT TO BE A SOUTH SEA ISLANDS EXPLORER?

Do you want to ...

... discover what lies behind the
palm-fringed beaches of a tropical island paradise?

... explore **exotic islands** and see wonderful **wildlife?**

... meet a **variety of natives?**
If the answer to any of these questions is **YES**, then this
is the book for you. Read on...

1

YOU WILL LEARN how to survive on a South Seas island and that what at first sight looks like paradise isn't without its pitfalls. And you'll find out what happened to some of the people who came before you — some who lived to tell the tale, and others who weren't so lucky.

YOUR MISSION ...

SHOULD YOU CHOOSE TO ACCEPT IT, IS TO FIND OUT WHAT WONDERFUL BIRD THE FEATHER BELOW BELONGS TO. THREE FEET LONG AND GLISTENING METALLIC RED THAT REFLECTS AS IF LIT UP FROM INSIDE WHEN THE SUN'S RAYS HIT IT, THE FEATHER TURNED UP AT THE BOTTOM OF AN OLD DISPLAY CASE IN THE BERLIN MUSEUM. THERE WAS A LABEL THAT SAID "LUNGA ISLANDS: PACIFIC OCEAN." NOTHING MORE.

HERE ARE A FEW FACTS ... AND A FEW RUMORS YOU'VE PIECED TOGETHER.

EXPERTS SAY IT'S A TAIL PLUME.

SPECIAL RED FEATHERS ARE USED AS MONEY ON SOME PACIFIC ISLANDS, SO THIS ONE MIGHT WELL BE VALUABLE.

THERE IS A LEGEND IN THE LUNGA ISLANDS OF WAMBATEGWEA — "THE PLACE OF THE ANGELS," A HIDDEN VALLEY UP A VOLCANO FILLED WITH FANTASTIC ANGEL BIRDS.

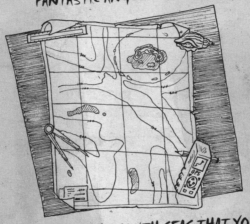

AN OLD TEXT ABOUT THE SOUTH SEAS THAT YOU FOUND IN THE MUSEUM'S ARCHIVES TALKED OF GLITTERING GOLDEN BIRDS THAT HAVE NO NEED FOR FEET BECAUSE THEY COME FROM HEAVEN AND NEVER NEED TO LAND.

STRANGE . . . BUT THE TRUTH MIGHT BE STRANGER. IT'S UP TO YOU TO FIND OUT. YOUR JOB, THE TRUSTEES OF THE MUSEUM SAID, IS TO TRAVEL TO THE REMOTE LUNGA ARCHIPELAGO AND DISCOVER (OR REDISCOVER) THE PARADISE BIRD WITH THE RED-GOLD PLUMES.

Unfortunately, disaster has struck. The boat you chartered foundered in rough seas. When it capsized you took to an inflatable dinghy and by the next morning, when the storm had cleared, you found yourself swept onto one of the islands.

Oceania, the South Seas

The vast Pacific Ocean is dotted with thousands of tiny and often widely spaced islands.

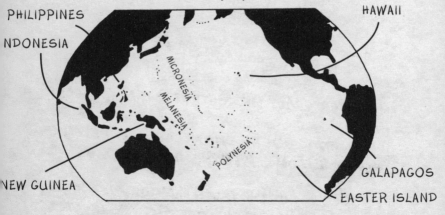

Polynesia — "the many islands," Melanesia — "the black islands" (because the people there have darker skin), and Micronesia — "the tiny islands," stretch up from Australia and New Guinea in the south to almost as far as Japan in the north, and eastwards a few hundred kilometers short of South America.

The islands are often made from the peaks of undersea volcanoes or the remains of coral reefs, and sometimes a mixture of the two. Many still have active volcanoes and are uninhabited. You might know the names of some of them, like Hawaii, Tahiti, and Fiji. Their names conjure up images of palm-fringed paradises, warm seas, nice beaches, and beautiful people. But what about the other islands, like the Tuamotus or the New Hebrides? What are they like? What would it be like to be washed up on one of them — no boat, no belongings — and have to survive? That's what this book is all about: tropical islands — how to survive on them and how to explore them. Read on....

The big thing to understand is how remote these islands are. For anybody, any animal, any plant to have gotten there means that it first had to cross thousands of miles of open ocean. Seeds, like coconuts, may have been swept there with the ocean currents; birds may have flown there. Land animals may have arrived on pieces of driftwood. Any people inhabiting the islands must have had amazing seafaring prowess to get there in the first place.

The result is that each island has its own unique community of animals and plants, and there won't be many types of each compared to the number on the main continents. There also won't be many big land animals.

COCONUT SEEDLING

Elephants and tigers are unlikely to find pieces of driftwood large enough to cling on to for an ocean crossing! Any animal much larger than a rat has most likely been introduced by man. That's not to say there aren't interesting creatures to find. Without competition from those big, fierce mainland animals, some of the island life has evolved into weird and wonderful forms found nowhere else on the planet like . . .

The Giant Tortoise (Galapagos)

Normally a peaceful plant eater, but not averse to a bit of cannibalism if it finds one of its own kind dead or dying.

The Dodo (Mauritius)

Now sadly extinct — a jumbo, flightless sort of killer pigeon.

The Kagu
(New Caledonia)

A bird that's lost the
inclination to fly.

The Komodo Dragon
(Komodo and Rinca islands: Indonesia)

A lizard with truly bad breath! The bacteria in its mouth
will make any wound it causes fester and stink.
So even if it just nips you, it can follow you later.
And you can't get away. You're on an island!

So what's it like on a tropical island? Well, that depends really
on where you are, how the winds blow, and where the ocean currents run. For Melanesia, Micronesia, and Polynesia, we're talk-
ing tropical; warm and humid with a fair smattering of rain pretty
well most of the year, except in the storm season, and then it
really rains.

7

When the winds blow up, the islands really take a pounding. Think about it. There are thousands of miles of open ocean with nothing in the way to stop the waves from getting really big. These waves lash the beaches ferociously while the winds rip into the rainforest behind. Super storms called cyclones are a fact of life here. Once in a while, often yearly, the winds have such force that they flatten the forest. Torrential rain causes landslides and flooding. There is nothing that animals and humans living here can do but seek shelter and sit the bad weather out.

You should've done that, too, when you heard the weather warning over your boat's shortwave radio! And you shouldn't have believed the man who sold you the yacht when he said she was unsinkable. She was breaking up and taking in water badly even before you hit the reef. You barely had time to press the auto-inflate for the life raft and pull yourself in before the hull broke in two. What happened after that is all a blur. Encased in

the orange plastic of the raft, pitched up, down, and sideways by waves you couldn't see, time lost any meaning. The storm seemed to last forever.

But now it is calm.

You are aware of the gentle lapping of waves, the sound of surf, the flapping of plastic sheeting in the breeze. Your face is wet. You taste salt in your mouth. You lie facedown on the orange plastic floor of the life raft that is swimming with water. You are alive and you have reached the shore. . . . Though which shore, you have no idea. . . .

Chapter 1
SHIPWRECKED

YOU CLAMBER OUT of the life raft onto gritty, white, coral sand. The beach curves into the distance on either side of you, edged only ten meters or so inland by coconut palm trees and a mass of luxuriant creepers that overspill the coastal jungle and tumble onto the beach.

Time to take stock of your situation.

There are no signs of people or animal life, except for the ticking of insects — maybe crickets — in the vegetation ahead of you. You know for certain that this island can't be Lunga Lunga, where you were heading before the storm.

There's no volcano behind the palm-fringed beaches. From what you can tell, scouting up and down the beach a short distance, this island is flat.

Perhaps as you explore further, you'll be able to work out where you've landed.

You're going to have to survive until help arrives. That'll mean living off what you can find. You've got a few things with you. Maybe you'll be able to put these to use. You spread your belongings across the sand. This is all you've got:

- Your clothes — T-shirt, shorts, plastic sandals.
- The contents of your pockets — a few coins, several banknotes.
- The inflatable life raft — punctured and ripped.

You have no food, nothing sharp you could use as a knife, and no means of making fire.

You'll need to consider how you can use those few belongings — along with things you'll find on the island, like driftwood, coral rock, and seashells — to help you survive.

Basic Survival

These are things you must consider...
Food, fire, shelter, water, signal (getting help/rescue).
Choose your answers from the list above.

1. Which is the most urgent one to sort out now?
2. Which one should you sort out last? Or, to put it another way, which is least important for your immediate survival?
3. Which one can help you with three of the others?
4. Coconut trees are common on this island. Which of these survival needs could they help you with?

(Answers on page 15)

To survive, you will need food, shelter, and most urgently fresh-WATER. If you don't drink soon you will become dehydrated. You will start to get headaches, feel ill, and it will seriously affect your ability to find food and sort out shelter. Too long without water and you will lose consciousness.

You can't drink seawater. You can distill it to get fresh water — boil it up, collect and cool down the steam — but to do that you'll need to make fire. Look at your surroundings. What can you get a drink from **right now?**

Yes. You've got it. COCONUTS!
Luckily there are a few fallen ones that will do for now, though they're probably old and the "milk" inside might not be that good. Getting them open might prove difficult, though. Here's how you can do it.

- Stick a wooden stake into the ground — try breaking a stick so it has a pointed end. If you can't, do as best you can with a blunt-ended one.
- Spike the coconut husk and pry off the fibrous coating. This takes some effort.
- When you get to the nut underneath, gouge through one of the "eyes" (you might manage this with a piece of stick, stone, or seashell). When you've drunk the "milk" inside, you can break open the nut and eat the flesh. The easiest way to do this is to hit it on the seam between the "eyes" with the larger "mouth" at the bottom (see right). The nut should break in two.
- *Note*: young, green coconuts hold the most liquid but have less flesh.

QUIZ

Coconuts can be a real lifesaver. If providing food and drink weren't enough, they have far more uses than that. Can you match up the use to the part of the plant?

1. White coconut flesh
2. Fibrous husks
3. Trunk
4. Fronds
5. Coconut "milk"
6. Shell

A. Soak them for a couple of weeks in seawater until they soften and go smelly, then twist the fibers into *sennit* rope. Making coconut fiber rope is a major money earner in tropical coastal areas around the world.

B. For food — you can also extract oil (using it for cooking with or lighting lamps) from it. Beware; too much flesh from old coconuts can give you diarrhea.

C. Building ... or burning as fuel.

D. Drink it. In young ones there's more but it's watery.

E. Make bowls, water-carrying pots, even spoons!

F. Weave them together to make roofing for your shelter.

(Answers on page 17)

There's another part that's well worth eating that you probably won't have thought of. It's called the palm "cabbage." It's at the top of the palm where the new fronds are sprouting. It's tasty and nutritious.

Now you can probably understand why the Samoan islanders call the coconut the "tree of life." They have at least seven sorts around their shores, each with their preferred uses, whether for food, a drink, or making *sennit* rope.

Once your supply of old "windfall" nuts has run out, you'll need to climb into the palms to get your coconuts. The best, healthiest coconuts don't fall out of the trees of their own accord. They have to be "helped." Look for small, slanted trees, which are going to be easier (and safer) to climb.

Shin up with your knees on either side; pull up with your arms and legs alternately. Better still, tie a strip of tough fabric or rope around your ankles and use that to help you climb up. For the cord, you could rip (or use a broken seashell to cut) a strip off your life-raft. Before you do so, remember you may have better uses for the life raft.

When you get to the top, twist off the nuts. You could also try to pull out the palm cabbage while you're up there.

Coconut milk will satisfy your thirst for the present, but to survive any length of time you are going to need a steady supply of fresh water — like a stream. It's clear you need to explore your island. You first need to find if there's a source of water, then search for things to eat and find a place and suitable materials to build a shelter.

You set off along the beach.

The island is small. Before midday you have walked all the way around. The bad news is that you found no stream, though you did find plenty of dry driftwood that might be useful for building a shelter or for making a fire. You've also seen fish, shrimps, and shellfish in the shallows, which might be useful for food if you could catch them.

Your island is at no point more that 400 meters wide. Coconut palm trees fringe the edges. Farther in is dense jungle with some tall trees (some have been blown down in the storm), thickets of bushes, and spiky palm trees.

The ground in the center of the island is swampy and there are some standing pools of water that haven't dried up since the storm. That's your water problem sorted out for the moment.

Apart from coconuts, there are other food plants here that you can use. Some of these will have seeded themselves naturally, their seeds blown in on the wind or washed in by the sea (this is how the coconuts got here).

Some seeds will have been brought in the droppings of passing birds. But some of the plants will have been introduced deliberately by people, like the breadfruit, which was often planted by passing seafarers as a source of food just in case they ever became shipwrecked at some later date.

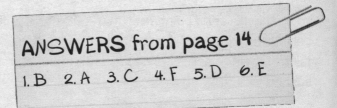

ANSWERS from page 14

1. B   2. A   3. C   4. F   5. D   6. E

Food for Thought – Quiz

Look at the pictures of these food plants, which you might come across. Match the plant and fruit to the way it is eaten.

1. Taro

2. Coconut

3. Breadfruit

4. Sago

A. Eat the flesh, drink the milk. It has a multitude of uses.

B. You can peel and eat the fruit raw (but you have to avoid the seeds and the rough bits as these can upset your stomach). It's better cooked; this also makes the seeds edible – starchy but filling!

C. Peel and cook – not unlike sweet potatoes or yams, which are also staple foods in the South Sea islands.

D. Chop down the tree and scoop out the pulp in the middle. Cook it up to make a starchy slop not unlike wallpaper paste.

Apart from coconuts, you can only find one of these food plants growing on your island. Look at the pictures in this chapter. Which is it?

(Answers on page 20)

There's an added bonus with sago . . .

Grubs!

Delicious little morsels of protein. Eat them raw or lightly fried — a mouthwatering, buttery taste; soft, squidgy, with a little crunch when you get to the mouthparts.

Note: When eating them live, watch out for those jaws as they can give you a nasty nip.

In any case, the delights of sago are something that will just have to wait. Even if there were sago palms on your island, you don't have the tools to cut them down, let alone get at the pulp inside. You'll have to satisfy your hunger with coconuts and raw, unappetizing breadfruit for the moment until you find something else. But while you're stuffing yourself, shouldn't you be thinking about something else?

Night will be upon you soon and look at those clouds on the horizon. . . .

The wind's whipping up.

You're going to need shelter.

ANSWERS from pages 18—19

The only food plant that grows here is breadfruit. There's a breadfruit tree in the picture of the island jungle on page 17.

1. C   2. A   3. B   4. D

Chapter 2
BEYOND JUST SURVIVAL

THE CLOUDS ARE still far enough away for you to have time to consider where to place your camp. For the moment you could just find somewhere sheltered and cover yourself with what remains of your life raft to keep the worst of the rain off, but you still have time to find yourself a more suitable campsite; remember, you could be stuck here for days, weeks . . . or even longer.

Think about what sort of place would be best to site your shelter. You'll want to be close to a source of freshwater. You'll need building materials such as wood and palm fronds for roofing. And you'll probably want a good view of the sea, too, so you can signal any passing boats or planes to rescue you. As there is no high land on the island, you may have to stay close to the seashore.

Take a look at the map of the island on the next page, which shows various areas where you might place your shelter. Each has an advantage and a disadvantage. Work out the advantage and the disadvantage for each.

Finding Shelter — Quiz

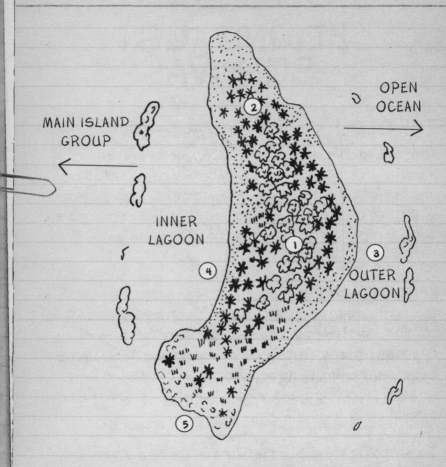

MAIN ISLAND GROUP

OPEN OCEAN

INNER LAGOON

OUTER LAGOON

SCRUB

JUNGLE

SAND

PALMS — COCONUT GROVES

ROCKY OVERHANG

Location

1. Central jungle
2. Coconut grove
3. Outer lagoon
4. Inner lagoon
5. Rock overhang by the sea

Advantage

A. Good source of palm fronds for making
   the roof of your shelter.
B. Good view of the sea.
C. Good view of the ocean.
D. Close to source of fresh water.
E. A natural shelter.

Disadvantage

V. Faces other islands, not the open ocean so there
   may not be passing ships.
W. A coconut could drop on your head.
X. If the sea washes in you could get trapped
   and drown.
Y. This place would face the full force of any storms.
Z. No view of the sea to look for passing boats.

(Answers on page 27)

So, which one would you choose? The inner lagoon is probably
your safest bet, though you'll have to transport building materials and water to your campsite.

Here's how you could construct a basic shelter.

ROOF MADE FROM PALM LEAVES LAID OVER THE FRAME. WHEN YOU HAVE MORE TIME YOU COULD WEAVE THE FRONDS TOGETHER FOR EXTRA STRENGTH AND WEATHERPROOFING.

RAISE YOUR BED FROM THE GROUND TO KEEP DRY AND TO KEEP THE BUGS OUT. YOU COULD MAKE YOUR LIFE RAFT INTO A HAMMOCK OR A POLE BED ... BUT THINK! THAT BRIGHT ORANGE PLASTIC MIGHT COME IN REALLY USEFUL FOR SOMETHING ELSE LATER.

FRAMEWORK CAN BE MADE FROM THIN PALM TRUNKS AND DRIFTWOOD. (WITHOUT A KNIFE OR MACHETE, YOU WON'T BE ABLE TO CUT YOUR POLES, THOUGH YOU MAY BE ABLE TO BREAK THEM OVER CORAL ROCKS OR FALLEN PALM TRUNKS.)

You wake up damp, cool, and unpleasantly insect-bitten. Yes, even paradise has mosquitoes.

The night was surprisingly cool and condensation coats your palm leaf shelter. Licking it off gives you a satisfying drink of pure water. You break into another coconut. Its flesh goes some way to satisfy your hunger, but you know that if you stay here for any length of time, coconuts and breadfruit will not keep you going. Nor will puddle water from the forest or condensation on palm leaves be enough to drink once the weather gets hot.

You need to think about how to get off the island or how to find help to get off. And if that doesn't happen immediately, you need to consider how to live off the land.

Here's how things stand at the moment:

- You're on a small, low-lying, uninhabited coral island somewhere in the Lunga archipelago. You don't know which island you are on — you've lost your map — but you do know that there are people living on some of the other islands in this group.
- You have very few possessions other than your punctured life raft and the clothes you abandoned your sinking boat with.
- You have taken care of your survival needs of food, water, and shelter for the moment. You do not have a fire.
- Fire is your next survival need. Use it to keep warm at night, cook the fish and shellfish you are going to catch, make smoke to keep the mosquitoes away — and to SIGNAL for help.

No matches. No lighter. No spectacles to use as a magnifying glass to focus the sun's rays. How can you make fire? Rub sticks together? It's not as easy as it sounds. Here's how the islanders of Samoa do it.

How to make fire: The fire plow

Cut a flat "hearth" stick and a thin "plow" stick with a flattened point at the end. Use a knife or something sharp, like a broken seashell, to plane up a curl of wood-shaving at the far end. Push the plow stick back and forth along the hearth stick, gradually going faster, turning the plow stick over occasionally. The idea is to first make a groove, then sawdust, which pushes up against the wood-shaving. The heat from the friction will eventually start the sawdust smoldering. You can then use some dry plant material, like the fibers from an old coconut husk, as tinder to make a fire, blowing on it gently until flames appear.

Sounds easy. It is not. This method could take days of trial and error of getting the plowing technique right, not to mention using the correct type of wood (in Samoa, they use dry hibiscus wood). These days most people prefer to use matches or cigarette lighters, which are far quicker, more convenient ways of making fire, but the fire plow method is still remembered . . . and still used.

One thing, though, once you've made fire, you'll want to keep it going. You don't want to go through all that palaver again when you see a sail on the horizon and you want to make a signal. So be prepared. Make sure you have plenty of fuel for your fire; enough to keep it smoldering (remember you will probably need to stay close to it), with some reserve fuel that you can pile on when you really want to get your signal fire going. Also remember, on a small island like this you will have to conserve your resources. Don't burn too much firewood. Go easy on the coconuts and breadfruit. You don't want to use them all up . . . this is exactly what happened on Easter Island.

Ecological Disaster on Easter Island

Famous for its gigantic carved stone heads, Easter Island at the far eastern end of Polynesia is now a windswept and treeless place. For years it was uninhabited.

But it wasn't always like that. The carved stone heads that litter the island and the numerous ruins are signs of a settled culture. There once lived here a skilled people who had the technology to work stone, then raise the huge blocks upright.

So what happened? Quite simply, the islanders outstripped their resources. They cut down their forests for wood and to make room to grow their crops, but on such a small island, the trees didn't grow back fast enough and the crops weren't enough to feed the people. The islands were too isolated for the inhabitants to travel anywhere else. Besides, they had cut down the trees so they had no wood to make boats . . .

People started fighting over the few resources that were left. Some turned to cannibalism. In the end, the people of Easter Island starved to death.

Trying to start a fire takes most of the rest of the day. Several times you manage to get the sawdust that your fire plow makes smoldering, but adding the glowing embers to some dry tinder and blowing on it to get a flame is much harder than you thought it would be. Finally, at the point where you are about to give up, SUCCESS. You tip your smoldering ball of shavings into an old coconut husk and WHOOMPF — some of the fibers burst into flame. You add some more dry fibers and soon you have a respectable fire going. A burst of emotion sweeps over you. You feel you are going to survive after all.

Signal fire set, it's time to get busy again. You could strengthen your shelter in case the storms that brought you here return. You could try to find something more interesting to eat. Only a day spent on this island and the coconut diet is starting to get you down. So is the solitude. The fact is, your state of mind is one of the key things to your survival. You are totally alone on a tiny island and now that you've achieved your immediate survival needs, you're likely to find life here incredibly boring unless you give yourself things to do. You will have to keep your spirits up. And one way to do that is to keep busy.

For a start, you're going to need some protein in your diet. The coconuts and breadfruit will provide carbohydrates to give you energy, but as the days go on, apart from the fact that the monotonous diet will get you down, you will need vitamins and minerals to keep healthy and protein — from meat, fish, or eggs — to keep your muscles built up, so your body can heal itself from any cuts and scrapes you get.

Good sources of protein on the island:

- Fish from the sea
- Prawns and shellfish
- Seabirds and their eggs
- Turtle eggs (at certain times of the year)
- Insects and grubs
- Land animals — there might be small rats or lizards living here

The problem is how to get this protein. As you haven't seen any sign of land animals or birds on the island, and the few insects you've seen look distinctly small or unappetizing (you're not that desperate yet), it looks like seafood is going to be on the menu. . . .

Here are some options that you could try:

- **Spearing** – make a harpoon and spear a fish . . . could take a lot of practice before you get it right.
- **Netting** – for this you'll need line to weave a net. You could use fibers from the spines of palm fronds, or if you have time (you may have lots of it!) twist together fibers from the husks of coconuts (it helps if you leave them to soak for a few weeks first).
- **Line fishing** – make your own hooks using thorns and splinters of wood. For line, you could cut strips from the bindings of your life raft.
- **Trapping** – many fish and octopuses will enter dark crevices in search of shelter or food. You could weave a container out of palm fronds, weight it down, add something for bait – preferably dead fish, though coconut flesh might do to begin with.

You could consider all these methods – it depends on how much time you spend on the island. How long will you have to survive on this island? What if you never get rescued? That's something not worth thinking about – you need to keep your morale up.

What about making a raft and getting out of here?

Note: Your original life raft is ripped beyond repair.

Look at this list and decide which items are FOR making a raft to sail away on and which are AGAINST.

	For / Against
1. Building materials — like tree trunks — available	
2. Unpredictable ocean currents	
3. You don't know where you are going	
4. Coconuts and breadfruit will store a long time	
5. Fresh water is hard to get	
6. No tools to make a seaworthy raft	

What do you think? Would you risk everything to get off this island or would you stick it out and hope for rescue? After all, you have everything here that you need to survive.

(Answers on page 32)

As the sun goes down that evening, you stare out to sea praying that someone will turn up. Far in the distance you catch sight of three birds. Two larger black ones with pointed wings and forked tails are swooping at a smaller bird, which skims the wave tops, laden down with something in its beak. The other two appear to be taking turns to dive and peck at the small bird until it spits out its burden, which is snatched out of the sky an instant before it hits the water. As the black birds squabble in midair over their prize, the smaller bird speeds away, the rays of the setting sun catching its long tail plumes for just a moment, lighting them up a bright fire red.

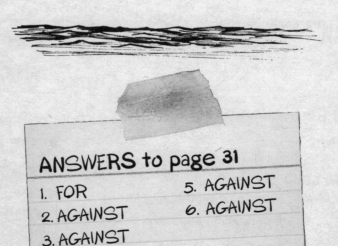

ANSWERS to page 31

1. FOR
2. AGAINST
3. AGAINST
4. FOR
5. AGAINST
6. AGAINST

Chapter 3
SAMSON LATI TO THE RESCUE

MORE RAIN LAST night. Getting fresh drinking water has not been the problem you anticipated. And your shelter has held up. What's more, now that you've gotten used to living here, you remember to cover up your firewood, so that's still dry. You don't keep the fire going all the time anymore. After a lot of practice with different types of wood, you found a combination of plow and hearth that works really well in your fire plow. Provided you've got dry tinder (fibers from the inside of coconut husks are really good for this. Ripped-up banknotes work well, too!) you find you can now get a fire lit reasonably easily.

If making fire has kept your spirits up, then the food has brought you down. So has the boredom. You've tried spearfishing, but that's been a waste of time and effort since anything worth eating has seen you coming and swum off. All the protein you've found so far has been from capturing a crab you found under a rock (it tried to nip you but you pried it out with a stick in the end), and a few large grubs that you found inside some strange palm fruit that you discovered in the forest.

Still, you have found useful building material — fronds from pandanus palms, which you've found are tough enough to braid together to use as ropes.

And this morning you made a discovery. . . .

Footprints. And they're not yours. At first you thought you'd probably walked around the island and found your own trail, but these prints are wider than yours. The tracks were on one of the beaches on the other side of the island. There were also a couple of long indents that may have been made by a boat being beached. It's hard to tell. The tracks went into the trees to a pandanus palm and came back. It looked like some leaves had been stripped off the palm. Maybe the person had taken the fronds to make some repairs to the boat.

Whoever it was, you missed them. You rush to your fire-lighting materials and hastily start plowing. Maybe there's a chance that the person might see the smoke from a fire even if they're out of view. Once the fire's roaring, you heap on some damp leaves. That makes it really start to smoke.

White smoke . . . of course black smoke would show up more against the sky. You could burn the remains of your plastic life-raft. That would make dark smoke . . . but if your signal didn't work, you could have used up an important survival item.

You wait.

And wait.

And wait.

Nothing.

Then you see it... canoe. Or is it two...? No, it's only one with an outrigger float to stabilize it on one side. And one person. Heading your way.

You rush down onto the beach, grabbing your orange plastic life raft, which you'd been using as your bed. Whoever's in the canoe is bound to see that if you wave it around.

The person in the boat has seen you. He's waving back. He lines the canoe up with the waves, holding it still for a moment, then rides in on the surf.

He looks a bit embarrassed by your hugs and handshaking.

"Good fella mornen long yu. Yu oraet?"

His language is strange. It sounds like English, but it's all mixed up.

"'Yu oraet?' Is that, 'You all right?'?"

You nod.

A huge smile comes over his face.

"Mi Samson Lati. Watkaen nem blong iufala nao?"

"Me Samson Lati. What kind of name belong you fellow now?"
(What is your name?)

What is he going on about? What language is this? Not English, as you know it. This is pidgin English, the dialect of the islands. It's English that's been added to with words from the island languages and changed slightly over the last 200 years. But you should be able to make yourself understood.

"Iufala boat tek me away."

And pretty soon you convince Samson to take you to his village.

How to speak pidgin English

Here are a few other phrases in pidgin English that might prove useful:

"Howmas longwe nao?" — "How much long way now?"
or "How far is there to go?"

"Tanggio Tumas." — "Thank you very much."

"No waris." — "You're welcome. No worries."

And if you had an upset tummy you might have **"bel-eran"** . . . you work that out.

Easy, isn't it? Now can you work out what these sentences mean?

(It helps if you read them out loud.)

1. "Me no savi."	A. "The time is 4 o'clock."
2. "Waswe taem nao?"	B "What is the time?"
3. "Taem hem save foa klok."	C. "Please. Where is the toilet?"
4. "Desfala blong iufala."	
5. "Plis. Smol house him I wea?"	D. "I don't understand."
	E.. "This is yours."

(Answers on page 41)

Samson Lati sits in the front of his canoe, pushes off into the gentle waves that lap onto the coral sand beach, starts paddling, and you're off. Once he's paddled past the white surf of the breakers at the edge of the coral reef, Samson hoists a small cloth sail, and you set off on the open sea.

This might worry you. There is no sign of land — how does Samson know where he's going?

Study the picture below.
Does it give you any clues?

Things to Look Out For

The direction of the "swell"

· Polynesian navigators are aware of the direction of the waves in different regions of the sea. They can also tell the faint ripple of wave reflections from islands when waves have hit land and bounced back off.

· **Fluffy white cumulus clouds** — these are often an indication of land — water evaporates over forest and then condenses into clouds.

· **Sun** — it's possible he's working out his direction from the sun's position. We're in the Southern hemisphere. The sun rises in the east, sets in the west, and is due north (hard to tell because it's nearly overhead) at midday — to do this, it helps if you know the time. And Samson doesn't have a watch.

· **Seabirds** — this might mean nothing, but many birds, like gulls and terns, stay fairly close to land.

· **Other factors** — the direction of the wind, sea currents, the smell of the breeze, some inner sense... all could play a part.

And at night...

The stars — their positions at various times of the night and where they set, let the sailor navigate from "star to star." Sometimes the navigators made charts out of palm fibers with shells tied on to map out these star paths.

The ocean glows — in some places, lights can be seen deep in the sea. The Polynesians call this "Te Lapa" — underwater lightning. It's caused by certain types of plankton glowing, a phenomenon known as bioluminescence. Sometimes "Te Lapa" is seen in lines, which show the direction of currents, and gives an indication of how far away land is.

Large ships often stir up luminous plankton with their propellers. There is a story of an American aviator in the Pacific during World War II who, low on fuel, followed the undersea lights all the way to his aircraft carrier, where he landed safely.

This knowledge has been used for centuries. This is how the tiny, vastly separated islands of the South Seas became populated; small groups of people in open sailing canoes taking to the oceans to find new land to live on.

Samson says he rarely gets lost when he's sailing around the Lunga islands. He can tell by the "feel" of the sea where he is. It's just as well because he's a fisherman and needs to know where the best tuna and lobster are to be found. He says you're lucky he found you because he rarely comes this far away from the main island group, but another man told him there was good fishing here so he decided to check it out. He shows the sleek, silvery bodies of three large fish he has caught. These will fetch a good price at the market, he reckons. If he hits the right sea currents and the wind is right, he should get back to his village tonight . . . or maybe the next morning. He shrugs, holding his hand up to judge the direction of the breeze.

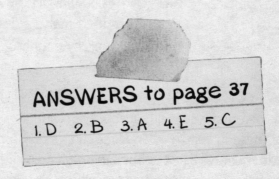

ANSWERS to page 37

1. D   2. B   3. A   4. E   5. C

QUIZ — DANGERS AT SEA!

So what are the hazards of the sea crossing? Match the hazard with what could happen.

Hazard	Possible consequence
1. Ocean currents.	A. The boat becomes tangled up or damaged in a collision.
2. Squalls, storms, erratic winds.	B. Could send you off course.
3. Shark attack.	C. Could send you off course or capsize your boat.
4. Floating trees and debris after storms.	D. Extreme danger — less so if you remain in the boat and don't make a disturbance such as by paddling.

(Answers on page 45)

Colliding with floating trees is not a danger you might normally think of. If you are vigilant and watch where you are going, you should be able to avoid them. Here's the story of someone who didn't....

An English aid-worker in the Solomon Islands, Will Randall, borrows an outboard-powered dugout canoe to take some fruit to sell in the market at a village on the neighboring island. It should be a routine trip. He has made the journey several times before and he is relaxed, daydreaming, standing at the stern of the boat, hand on the outboard motor's throttle, powering forward across a calm sea. The next moment he is pitched overboard. The boat has hit a submerged tree trunk. What is worse is that his boat is still going. Its throttle control is faulty, and set on full power. The canoe carries on in a straight line . . . into the distance and out of sight.

Will treads water and tries not to think of the sharks, which are common in this area. He kicks off his shoes. And his trousers . . . and with them slip off his underpants, too. This will be embarrassing, he thinks, if someone comes to rescue him.

By the submerged trunk there are some floating coconuts. Will grabs several for extra buoyancy and starts swimming in the direction his boat went. Eventually he arrives at an island. It is tiny, just 200 meters long, but it has enough vegetation that should provide food, shelter, and water.

Will survives on coconuts and waits for a boat to come past that he can signal to rescue him. The hardest part is the boredom when his mind wanders to what might happen if no help arrives.

Two days later, the driver of a passing motorboat spots Will and he is rescued. When he gets back to his village, it turns out no one was really worried about him. The sort of silly accident he had happens fairly often. The part of the story they keep reminding him of, though, is how shocked his rescuers were motoring past an island and seeing a man jumping up and down and waving at them with no clothes on.

And the boat? It just kept on going. It was found in some mangroves just a few hundred meters to the side of the village on the island where Will had been heading.

The day wears on. Samson expertly keeps the sailing canoe on what you know must be a bearing straight for his island.

By afternoon a smudge of green appears on the horizon, this revealing itself to be several low islands with a higher hazy outline of a mountain farther beyond them. The shape of the mountain is unmistakable; it's Lunga Lunga — location of your quest for the angel bird whose feather you looked at, what seems so long ago now, in the museum.

Perhaps when you get to Samson's village and equip yourself, you'll be able to continue your expedition. And who knows? Samson might be able to help you.

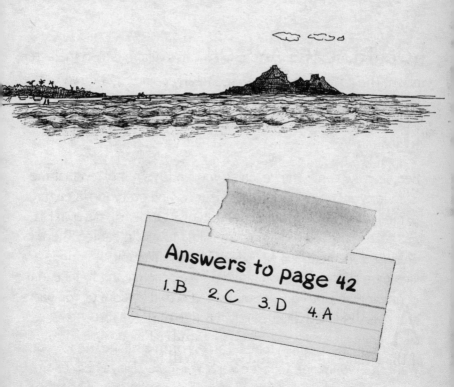

Answers to page 42

1. B   2. C   3. D   4. A

45

Chapter 4
CARGO CULTS AND FEATHER MONEY

YOU REACH SAMSON Lati's village late in the afternoon. The palm-thatched houses nearly come right down to the sea, and the narrow strip of white sand in front is covered with beached canoes and nets and piles of small fish left in the sun to dry.

People crowd onto the beach as you land. It's not often that the islanders of Lunga Tumaku get visitors, and everyone is eager to meet you. Samson is shouting things to them in his own language, not the pidgin English he talked to you in earlier. There is one word you hear him say several times. "Wantok." It sounds a bit like "One talk," and as you stand on the beach trying to take in the confusion around you, presently, the crowd in front of you parts and a very old man walks slowly through to greet you.

He is Tuai, the Bigman (chief/father) of this village. He is your Wantok — your "one talk," he says. Wantoks always help each other. That is the Kastom (custom). Tuai remembers when the

ALL ACROSS THE SOUTH PACIFIC THERE ARE ISLANDERS WHO IDENTIFY WHERE THEY COME FROM WITH SPECIAL MARKS OR SCARS, AND TATTOOS ON THEIR FACES AND ARMS.

Americans were here in the big war and he can speak your language. He can be your interpreter. Questions come thick and fast from the crowd.

"Where are you from?"

"Do you like our islands?"

"Do you want some food?"

"A bed for the night?"

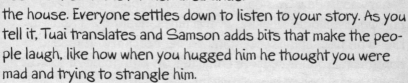

You are seated at one of the houses, brought a young coconut to drink from and fish and stodgy yam, which has been cooked in the kitchen area under the house. Everyone settles down to listen to your story. As you tell it, Tuai translates and Samson adds bits that make the people laugh, like how when you hugged him he thought you were mad and trying to strangle him.

The villagers know about the bird you are trying to find. They say hundreds of them live on the cliffs of a canyon on Lunga Lunga, though no one has landed on that island in living memory.

47

Bad things happened there. Many people died and now it is *tabu* to go there. Tabu (Taboo) means "forbidden" or "sacred." It's a Polynesian word that's entered the English language.

The islanders call the bird you are looking for the "bosun bird" because sometimes, like a bosun — the steersman on a ship — the bird flies in front of their sailing canoes as if showing them the way. The bird is all white with a long tail that shines like fire, but this is not the one whose feathers are used for money. Those feathers come from a small bird called a honeyeater that lives in the jungle on some of the islands. They are trapped by putting sticky resin on branches. A few feathers are plucked and if possible the honeyeaters are released again. The feathers are woven into belts made of brown pigeon feathers nine meters long. They used to be used as the dowry a man had to pay to a girl's family when he married her. On other islands, money made from cowrie shells or dolphin teeth is used, though these days the "bride-price" is more often paid in banknotes . . . or occasionally in pigs to eat at the wedding feast.

But what about the old stories of birds with no feet?

The islanders look at you as if you've gone mad, all except Tuai. "That was in New Guinea," he says. The people there used to sell European sailors the skins of the fantastically colorful birds found on that island. They took the feet off first. The sailors thought they must be birds from heaven with no need to ever land, so they called them "birds of paradise."

"The angel bird of your quest," he says, "it definitely has feet."

You spend three relaxing days at Lunga Tumaku, eating well, exploring the island, and finding out more about the local customs. Every couple of months, you are told, a trading ship comes by the island; that's when everyone gets their news and trades their copra (dried coconut kernels) to buy manufactured goods.

There's an airstrip behind the village but now it is grown over. Samson explains that the people thought that if they built a runway, airplanes would land and they would receive lots of gifts — "cargo," they call it. Other villages built docks to receive ships or marched in parades with homemade rifles. They had seen soldiers and sailors bringing money and gifts during World War II and they thought that if they did the right thing, they too would share in the bounty like the many black American soldiers they had seen. On one island the villagers had even gone so far as to slaughter all their pigs for a big feast, then were disappointed and very hungry when the "cargo" did not arrive.

This type of worship is called a cargo cult and has been going on since Christian missionaries arrived over 200 years ago. Many islanders in the Solomons and New Hebrides await the arrival of their savior, John Frum, who, they believe, will bring a time of prosperity. They believe that by preparing the way for ships or aircraft to land, then one day the gods will bring them their "cargo."

After three relaxing days you are eager to restart your expedition to find the angel bird with the fantastic red tail feathers. Tuai says that the cargo steamer will arrive at Lunga Tumaku in a week's time so if you set off now, you should be able to complete your mission, get back to the island, and then return home. The trouble is getting to the island. No one is willing to come with you. Nor do you have any money to buy the provisions you need. Luckily for you, Samson is at hand to help out. He agrees to take you to Lunga Lunga, though he will not set foot on the island. What's more, he will lend you some money to buy the provisions you will need.

Samson lends you fifty Vatu. Here's what you can get at the village market. Choose what you will buy.

☐ Lighter	10	
☐ Parang (big knife)	20	
☐ Candles	10 for 10	
☐ Cans of food	20 for 4 cans	
☐ Yams	10 for 20 yams	
☐ Taro pancakes	10 for 20 pancakes	
☐ Coconuts	10 for 20	
☐ Plastic sheet	10	
☐ String/rope	10	
☐ Light with batteries	20	
☐ Freshly caught fish	10	
☐ Fruit — pineapples	10 for 10	

You notice that some of the women selling things have dark red mouths and there are little patches of red spit near them. Don't worry; their mouths are not bleeding. The women are chewing Betel nut, which has a slight drug effect like smoking cigarettes. It turns their saliva red. They spit out the chewed-up nut mixture from time to time.

You take your purchases back to Samson. Let's see how good your choices were. Add up your points score.

Lighter	5	You know how to make a fire plow.
Parang	20	A "must."
Candles	5	Quite useful.
Cans of food	10	This food won't spoil, but only four cans won't go very far.
Yams	10	Good to fill you up but bulky to carry.
Taro pancakes	20	Light and easy to store.
Coconuts	0	You can find these for free.
Plastic sheet	7	You can always use palm thatch for a shelter.
String/rope	7	Useful for shelter making, but Samson will know some natural alternatives, such as strips of bark from certain trees.
Light with batteries	5	Useful but not essential.
Freshly caught fish	0	Samson is a fisherman. Besides, your fish will very quickly go bad in the tropical heat.
Fruit — pineapples	5	The taste of sugary fruit will raise your spirits, but fruit is bulky and heavy, considering the amount of energy it gives you.

Your Score

40 points and over	You've got it. Samson slaps your back and says what a fine explorer you are. Just one thing — couldn't you have bargained a bit harder to get some discount?
30 points	Fine, but you need to think ahead about what you can easily carry.
20 points	Samson shakes his head, takes your purchases, and starts off back to the market stalls to try for some refunds.
10 points	Go back home on the next steamer that calls by this island.

Fourth morning. With Samson's canoe loaded up you set off. The jagged peaks of Lunga Lunga loom in the distance. Samson is not his usual smiley, happy self as you draw near the mangrove forest that grows out into the sea along the island's southern edge.

The island is *tabu*. Many people died there.

Tuai's words repeat in your head.

Why — was it disease, headhunters, cannibals that caused the deaths? You will soon find out.

Chapter 5
BETWEEN THE SEA AND THE LAND

THE PEAKS OF Lunga Lunga stick up through the rainforest and mangroves ahead of you. Samson describes the mangroves as a forest that grows over the sea. He says he can tie up his canoe and wait for you there but he will not set foot on the island.

"Bad place him.
Blong spirits.
Bad people illness.
Many people die."

The sea journey to the island is quite rough until you reach the reef that fringes the island. Here it's so shallow that in places the canoe scrapes on the bottom. You and Samson have to get out and guide the boat, being careful not to tread on any sea urchins or poisonous stonefish that could be hiding among the coral. What makes this harder are the breaking waves that slide the boat and you along, then immediately pull you back with a strong undertow.

There are three main types of island here in the Lunga archipelago:

- **Active volcano.** Coral reefs grow up around the edges.
- **Dormant volcano,** which has sunk down over the years, leaving the coral as a fringing reef around the edge.
- **Coral atoll.** Once the volcano has disappeared entirely you are just left with the coral islands of the fringing reef.

Lunga Lunga is the second type of island.

2. FRINGING REEF —
DORMANT VOLCANO

1. ACTIVE VOLCANO

3. CORAL ATOLL

You have to get past fringing reef islands of old coral that stick above the present sea level. They sprout scraggy trees that are covered with nesting birds. When the wind shifts in your direction you can tell what much of these islands is made of. **Guano.** That's a nice way of putting it. The whole surface of these islands is bird poo. Actually, it's pretty valuable stuff. Chemicals in it called nitrates make excellent fertilizer. Some islands have been dug out and sold at great profit (to people, not to the birds who lost their stinky home).

RED-FOOTED BOOBY

Some of the birds here are frigate birds, the same pointy-winged black predators that you saw terrorizing a smaller bird a week earlier when you were stuck on the island. They wheel above and around your canoe, swooping frighteningly close; their 25-meter wingspans momentarily blot out the sun as they pass above you. With their long hooked beaks and black cloak wings they look menacing, but Samson says not to worry. He throws in the air a small fish he's caught and instantly it's pounced on by two frigates who tussle midair before the larger of the birds gets a good grip and whooshes up to enjoy his meal.

That's how they get their meals, Samson says. They don't catch fish for themselves. They just hassle other birds until they drop or throw up what they've caught. The frigates catch it before it hits the water.

Frigate Birds — Pirates of the Air

The bonuses of being a frigate bird:

- Pointed wings and swallowtail give excellent control to loop and swoop and grab that puked-up fish before it hits the water.
- Hooked tip to beak — extra grip for the food, plus useful for pecking at other birds to make them give up their hard-earned fish.
- Bright-red inflatable throat sack (males only) — for impressing the ladies.

The drawbacks of being a frigate bird.

Being supremely aerobatic comes at a cost!

- Tiny legs set well back along the body mean that you can't land on the ground or really walk along.
- No waterproofing on feathers. If you hit the water, you're going to stay there!

Finally, you are through the fore reef and paddling through a calm lagoon toward the forest that grows over the sea.

MANGROVES are trees that grow at the margin of the land and the sea. They have to be able to suffer salt levels that would kill less hardy plants. To do this, they grow a strange variety of tangled roots — stilt roots that stick up or snake through the mud. . . .

- **Air-absorbing roots** — nearest the sea.
- **Prop roots** branching out from the trunk. These trap mud brought in by the tides. The seeds germinate before they fall off the tree. Some of them fall off and land with the root already sticking into the mud so they can start growing straight away.
- **Knee-roots** — this type is found farther inland.

AIR-ABSORBING ROOTS PROP ROOTS KNEE-ROOTS

Between the forest clumps snake winding channels. Here the air is still and humid and filled with mosquitoes.
There are patches of mud and quicksand where, if you trod, you might never get out.

This is not quite sea and not quite land, as shown in the weird creatures that live here. Mudskippers are fish that spend most of their time out of water. They have eyes on the top of their head, and stiffened fins to help them walk-slither over the mud. Some can even climb trees.

You see crabs scuttling among the prop roots of the trees, and some speed into holes in the mud, cover themselves over, and wall themselves in as you approach. On some of the open areas of mud you can see their tracks and also tiny balls of mud laid out in patterns and lines. Crabs again. They sieve the mud through their mouthparts for any living matter. Every five mouthfuls or so, they deposit a ball of sifted mud on the ground and start all over again. There are crabs here that eat mud, some that burrow into it, some that sleep in the trees. Here are some facts you should know — but which are false? You decide.

A Crabby Quiz — True or False?

1. The robber crab, forty-five cen-
timeters long and up to two and a
half kilograms in mass, is also
known as the coconut crab as its
claws are so strong it can break
into coconuts.

2. Like crickets, some crabs can
make noises by rubbing their
legs together.

ROBBER CRAB

3. Male fiddler crabs have one over-
size claw so they can signal to
each other.

4. Amorous male fiddler crabs
can change color,
rather like chameleons.

FIDDLER CRAB

5. Hermit crabs don't have their
own shell so they use
empty seashells.

6. Some crabs migrate in the
millions, much like wildebeest
in the Serengeti or
starlings in
northern Europe.

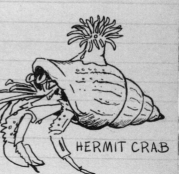

HERMIT CRAB

(Answers on page 60)

ANSWERS to page 59

1. **False.** Though they are called "Coconut crabs," the cracking reputation is just a myth! Though it's true that robber crabs do eat coconuts that have already been broken by falling or gnawed into by rats. Some scientists tested the robber crabs' coconut-cracking ability by putting some crabs in a closed area with just coconuts to eat. The crabs starved to death.

2. **True.** Ghost crabs have ridges on the edges of their claws, which they rub on one of their joints to make squeaks and croaks.

GHOST CRABS

3. **True.** They warn other males away and attract females in a sort of crab semaphore.

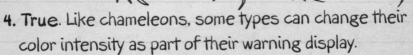

4. **True.** Like chameleons, some types can change their color intensity as part of their warning display.

5. **True.** But they don't always use shells. Some types of hermit crabs use tubes of bamboo or reeds for protection. Note: Hermit crabs should really be called hermit lobsters because that's what they are more closely related to.

6. True. On Christmas Island in the Indian Ocean, millions of scarlet land crabs swarm to a couple of beaches once a year. The males arrive first, dig burrows, and wait for the females to mate with. Then they return to their forest home, leaving the females to wait for the fertilized eggs to mature — a hundred thousand per crab — for the next two weeks. Then it's egg-laying time. The females have to dump their eggs in the sea either by going right into the water (which is risky, as these are land crabs and they can't swim), or by dropping them over a cliff edge. Many tumble and are swept away in the waves. And of the few eggs (later hatchlings) that survive the fish, moray eels, and other predators waiting to gobble them up, most will never get back to Christmas Island, as they won't be swept up with the right ocean current. That current only happens every six years or so and most years the entire spawning of a hundred million crabs is entirely wasted.

Samson paddles the canoe, punting off the shallow mud. The stabilizing outrigger is a hindrance here. A narrow canoe would let you travel farther down the channels.

Eventually the channel is so narrow it's clear that the boat will go no farther. Solemnly Samson hands you the parang and his tree-bark string bag filled with your provisions. You're going to have to wade through the mud and clamber over the roots the rest of the way to dry land. He'll wait here until you come back. If you don't return in two days . . . well, he'll make that decision then if it comes to it.

Without looking back, you set off. Within minutes you are covered in mud, bitten by mosquitoes, sweating fom the exertion in the heat and humidity. As much as possible you try to tread where there are lots of roots so as not to sink in. In places you are knee-deep in mud. When you have to cross the channels, the water comes up to your waist. Sometimes you sink farther into the mud and the water comes even higher. When you stop for a rest, you are aware of your own labored breathing, the whine of mosquitoes, the lapping of the water, and the scraping of branches rubbing together. You hear a rustle in the twigs and something plops into the water. You realize you are not alone in the swamp!!!!

Chapter 6
TABU, HEADHUNTERS, AND CANNIBALISM

YOU HOLD YOUR breath, trying to fix where the noise came from. There are predators here: snakes, crocodiles, even some sharks that hunt far down the mangrove channels. With your feet sinking in the mud, you stand little chance if any large predator is around, but is it better to stay still and quiet where you are or to keep on moving?

Here are some of the predators in the mangroves. Try to match each one with the risk they pose.

PREDATOR

1. Saltwater crocodile
   (up to six meters or more)

2. Mangrove monitor lizard (around one meter long)

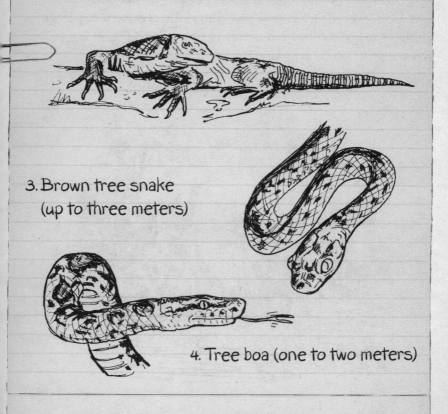

3. Brown tree snake
   (up to three meters)

4. Tree boa (one to two meters)

RISK

A. Little risk. It's a constrictor, which means it kills by wrapping itself around its prey. As most are only around a meter and a half long, there's no point in its trying to crush you.

B. More of a scavenger than a killer, though if you were lying around injured and unconscious (or asleep) it might take a bite.

C. Truly dangerous. Only found on some of the westernmost Pacific islands.

D. Poisonous but its fangs are at the back of its mouth. It would have to open really wide to inject the venom. Would you be so stupid as to annoy it that much?

(Answers on page 68)

Actually, compared to rainforests around the rest of the world, these island jungles contain few large, dangerous animals. They are too remote for these animals to have traveled there. The saltwater crocodile is only found in western Pacific islands near New Guinea and, generally, the farther east and more remote the islands become, the fewer large animals there are. On one island the main predator is a snail. Yes, a snail — and not a very big one at that. . . .

The story of poor Partula and the killer snail

Partula is a small, harmless snail that lives on the island of Tahiti in French Polynesia. It lives a relaxed and harmless life in the jungle there, chomping on leaves and generally getting on peaceably with the ecosystem around it. But someone had a great idea. How about we introduce giant African edible snails for people to eat? You don't have to look after them. They grow huge (their shell 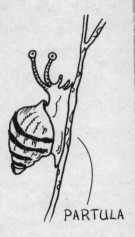 is a little bit larger than your fist) and they don't move fast so you can just pick them off the trees and presto! A ready meal for two.

PARTULA

The giant African land snails liked the forest on Tahiti. They liked it so much that they multiplied and multiplied. Pretty soon they were a pest, eating every plant in sight. Now that there was less food to eat, the snails that had lived there to begin with, the Partulas, began to die out.

GIANT AFRICAN SNAIL

So the people who had introduced the giant African snails had another great idea. Let's introduce some meat-eating "wolf" snails to keep down the numbers of the giant snails. They'll be the snail equivalent of guided missiles, the kind you can "fire and forget."

WOLF SNAIL

Now you have to look at it from the point of view of the "Hit-snails." Why bother with a huge, tough African giant when you can knock off a peaceful Partula with half the effort? The guided missile snails headed straight for the Partulas. Now they are nearly extinct.

Sadly, the story of the Partula snail, or a story like it, is being repeated all over the Pacific. Island animals are being wiped out by "introduced" animals like rats, cats, and brown tree snakes, which find them easy pickings compared to their prey on the continents where they originated. For example, many island birds, like the Aldabra white-throated rail in the Indian Ocean, have lost the ability to fly, as it's not worth the effort if there are no predators to get away from. Also they nest on the ground and make no effort to hide their eggs. Aldabra rails are now endangered. Other species like the barred-wing rail have become extinct.

ALDABRA
WHITE-THROATED RAIL

1. C   2. B   3. D*   4. A

*Brown tree snakes don't just climb trees. They rather like slithering up electricity towers, too. On the island of Guam, they have caused hundreds of power outages when they cause short-circuits between power lines and the metal of the towers. This, incidentally, fries the poor snake.

Eventually you make it to dry land. The stilt-rooted mangroves gradually give way to straight-trunked rainforest trees and palms and the land starts to rise ahead of you. Samson has said that to find the valley where the angel birds live, you just have to find the stream that leads into the mangroves and follow that toward its source. Of course you can't trust his directions that much. Samson wouldn't come with you onto Lunga Lunga Island. He said the place was tabu — forbidden.

But why would that be? As you take a moment to rest and take a drink from the stream, your mind goes through the possibilities. One reason might be that the island was deserted because of disease.

Maybe there was malaria (spread by mosquitoes) here and the people decided to move to a healthier island.

Maybe the people were afraid of the *Kakamoras*, the wild pygmies who are said to live in the mountain jungles of some of the islands. Only one to one and a half meters tall with long straight hair down to their waists, they supposedly jabber unintelligibly, have the strength of three men, and, legend has it, steal village women to take back to their caves.

Maybe Lunga Lunga was deserted because of headhunting? On many Pacific islands, tribes would send out raiding parties to capture slaves and to take heads. It was believed the life force of a person was in his head and that you gained their power if you had theirs. The skulls of warriors were useful as offerings to bring luck and goodwill from the gods, for instance, when launching a new war canoe, building a house, or when burying a dead tribal chief. Headhunting cost the lives of huge numbers of the coastal people who had to spend their lives on constant lookout for the raiding parties. One way of telling the good or bad intent of an approaching canoe was to look at the carved wooden figurehead on its prow. This was often of a man or a dog holding either a dove or a skull. If the figure was holding a skull, then it was time to run away to the hills.

It was mainly men whose heads were taken. Sometimes their bodies were eaten. Women and children were usually captured as slaves.

You're about to explore an island that's tabu. Let's hope you don't suffer the same fate as the Austrian explorer Von Foullon Norbeeck and his three friends when they tried to climb Mount Tatve on Guadalcanal, one of the Solomon Islands. The mountain was tabu to the local people. They said that if the explorers climbed it, then all the villagers would die. The islanders killed all four of the explorers. Two they ate!

And what does human flesh taste like? Rather like pork — or so they say. The islanders of the New Hebrides and of New Guinea in the western Pacific call their human victims "long pig" because they say pigs and humans look (and taste) much the same when prepared for eating!

Maybe there was another reason why lots of people died here, something far more recent. You push through into a clearing in the forest. This is what you find. . . .

Pulling away some of the creepers reveals the corroded fuselage of an airplane. Those rusted stumps pointing out of the wings must once have been machine guns.

There are three skulls nearby. Someone has obviously placed them there . . . some time ago, judging from the way vegetation has grown around them.

The Pacific islands were the scene of some of the bloodiest fighting during World War II. First invaded by the Japanese, then retaken by the Americans, tropical island paradises like Guadalcanal in the Solomon Islands and Truk in the Gilberts became scenes of carnage and devastation.

As American forces island-hopped toward Japan through the Solomons, the Carolines, and the Marianas, the Japanese retreated and sometimes men got left behind. This happened to Sergeant Shoichi Yokoi. He was stationed on Guam. When the Americans landed in 1944, Shoichi Yokoi hid in the jungles and waited for them to arrive. Perhaps he would ambush them. But they didn't come . . . for a whole year . . . or the next . . . or for nearly thirty years more. In fact, the Americans didn't think the island's interior had much strategic value so they didn't bother going far into the jungle. The war ended and they all went home. But not Shoichi Yokoi. His orders were not to surrender, so he stayed, living off nuts, berries, frogs, snails, and rats, and clothing himself in beaten tree bark. It was not until 1972 that he was finally captured by two local hunters who told him the war had ended twenty-seven years earlier.

Shoichi Yokoi was not the only Japanese soldier to survive like this. Another, Lieutenant Hiroo Onada, hid in the Philippine jungles until 1974.

He kept his rifle in good order and killed several villagers. He was only persuaded to give himself up when his former commanding officer was flown out to tell him the war had ended and order him to surrender using a megaphone.

Could this be the reason why the island of Lunga Lunga is tabu? Could it be that there was so much killing during World War II that the people decided to move their villages to somewhere they could have peace?

Someone must have placed those skulls there. Headhunters? Probably not. If a man's life force is in his head, these were probably arranged like that out of respect for the dead.

You back away from the plane and the skulls. You are aware of the ground under you — squishy, slimy, and rather sweet-smelling. Lots of seeds litter the floor. *Thud* — you knock into a tree trunk.

What are all those dark bundles dangling from the branches? Perhaps they are some sort of strange fruit.

Fruit with eyes?

BATS!

Chapter 7
CLIFFS OF THE ANGEL BIRD

YOU STAND AS if frozen.

The bats hang upside down from any free space all over the branches of the tree. Most are hunched inside their black velvet-leathery wings, but some are twisting their heads out to look at you and sniff at the air. They are cat-size with foxlike muzzles full of sharp teeth. Each wing has a vicious-looking single claw. Some of the bats closest to you are using these to help them crawl along the branches.

You assess the situation ...

1. What sort of bats are these?	Vampires or Flying foxes?
2. What do you think they eat?	Fruit, insects on the wing, or animal blood?
3. Are they a danger to you?	Yes or No?
4. Why are they hanging from the tree?	Sleeping through the daylight hours or waiting to ambush their prey?
5. What should you do?	Stay still, edge away slowly, or run for it?

(Answers on page 74)

1. Flying foxes — also known as fruit bats. They are not closely related to the smaller insect-eating bats that give out high-pitched sound waves and listen to the echoes to find their way and hunt in the dark. Flying foxes rely on good night vision. And they have nothing to do with foxes; they got that name because of the shape of their faces.

2. Fruit (the ground was slimy with their poo and littered with seeds).

3. No danger. They eat fruit. You wouldn't be on their menu.

4. Sleeping through the day. At night they will fly off in search of fruit trees. They can be a pest to farmers.

5. Edge away slowly. Try not to scare them. When threatened, they rely on the confusion of lots of them taking to the air at once to discourage their attackers.

You weren't slow enough. The fruit bats take flight, the whole tree-full of them. The air is thick with terrified bats. You feel the gusts of air from their meter-wide wingspans blowing your face and hair. A bat brushes by your arm. Another hits you full in the chest and hangs from your T-shirt for a second by its hooked finger claw. You throw it to the ground and run.

A little while later, your composure regained, you head back to the stream and continue up the steep valley. Your route is becoming steeper now and more clogged with vegetation. You find yourself scrambling over moss-covered rocks and pushing through tree ferns and cycads that look more like relics from the age of the dinosaurs than modern-day plants. There are cliff walls rising above you to the left and right. A stream gushes from a gap between them. You are aware of the screaming calls of birds echoing between the rock walls. You scramble up and over the lip of a small waterfall; this is what you see . . .

The scene is spectacular with rock faces, edged top and bottom by prehistoric-looking jungle, and, filling the air, the angel birds of your quest. These are red-tailed tropic birds. Gull-size, they are pure white except for a black stripe above the eyes and a tail streamer that shines brightest scarlet when the sun reflects off it. Most of the time they are flying far out at sea, flying high, searching for squid and fish close to the surface, which they dive upon and catch.

You've discovered their nesting cliffs. The air is filled with their shrieking calls, from the nests on the ledges and crevices, and from birds in the air whose buoyant flight makes them look almost as if they are being pulled up by invisible strings. Some are hovering. Some even appear to be flying backward.

You've done it!

You've rediscovered the angel bird, the owner of the tail feather you found so long ago in the museum. And you've found not just one but hundreds, a whole nesting colony, in fact. This could be a real scientific breakthrough. What's more, you've made your discovery even after being shipwrecked on a deserted island and surviving that. You've had to learn how to find freshwater, forage for food, and make fire. How many people would have carried on with their mission after that ordeal?

You've shown such strength of character. A feeling of pride surges over you. What a story you'll have to tell when you get home! They might even make a movie about it. They're sure to want to send you back with a film crew to show the world the fabulous nesting cliffs . . .

when you get home!

Can you remember the way you came?

First, can you find your way back down through the jungle to the mangroves where Samson Lati is waiting for you with his outrigger canoe? Then, can you find your way back to his island and finally back to the island where you were shipwrecked? Look at the map and figure out which hexagons you passed through. There are several islands on the map. Can you figure out which one was yours?

(Answers on page 80)

79

ANSWER to page 78. The route back is:

H The nesting cliffs   E or K Sea
P The wrecked war-   L Sea
   plane and the   M or T Sea
   fruit bats   V Your island. Can you
I The mangrove swamp   spot the place where
C Frigate bird island   you made your camp?
D Samson Lati's island

80

You've survived life on a deserted island and proved yourself to be a skilled explorer. What next? What challenges await you? Have you thought about trekking through the **Himalayas**, exploring the **Desert**, or setting off on an expedition across the frozen **Arctic** wastes?

EXPLORERS WANTED!

Your mission...

should you choose to accept it, is to be the first person to reach the peak of Dangiroba, in the Himalayas.

Are you ready for the challenge?

Explorers Wanted to:

- Climb the highest mountains in the world
- Survive the icy cold
- Brave avalanches and sliding glaciers
- Encounter the legendary yeti
- Escape fanged deer and hungry bears

Includes the author's own expedition notes and sketches!

EXPLORERS WANTED!

IN THE HIMALAYAS

Simon Chapman

SO... YOU WANT TO BE A HIMALAYAS EXPLORER?

You want to...

...scale Dangiroba peak at the **"roof of the world"**?

...search for **snow leopards, yaks, and yetis**...?

...brave the most **fearsome mountain range on the planet**...?

If the answer to any of these questions is **YES**, then this is the book for you, so read on....

THIS BOOK WILL give you the lowdown on how to mount an expedition into the high Himalayas, from trekking through lush, forested valleys and over rocky passes to braving avalanches and crevasses as you climb through the snows to an untouched mountain peak. Along the way, you'll find out about some of the people who came before you, some who succeeded . . . and others who tried but failed.

YOUR MISSION, should you choose to accept it, is to be the first person to climb "Dangiroba." It's not the highest peak or even the hardest to climb but, like many summits, until now it has just been too out-of-the-way and difficult to get to. There are no roads within easy reach, and trekking on foot is the only option. Just getting there will be an adventure. There'll be rivers to cross, perilous cliff-edge trails to traverse, and then there are the dark, creepy forests, rumored home of the legendary beast-man, the yeti. Does it really exist? Maybe you'll be the one to find out!

You'll have to cross the infamous Lohtang pass and enter the isolated valley of Polpo, where the people herd yaks and drink their tea mixed with yak butter.

Finally, you'll attempt your ascent of "Dangiroba," climbing ice and rock so high up that you'll be gasping for breath at every step in the thin air. Watching out for avalanches that can sweep you away, you'll have to cross crevasse-strewn snowfields and then climb to the summit. It will be an adventure at the edge of human capabilities. Do you think you're up to the challenge?

Time to set the scene...

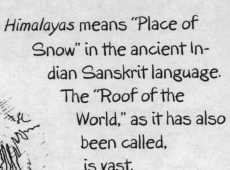

Himalayas means "Place of Snow" in the ancient Indian Sanskrit language. The "Roof of the World," as it has also been called, is vast.

The mountains range from Pakistan in the west right across the top of India, Nepal, and parts of China. There's more than just snowcapped summits. On the southern side, foothills that are fair-size mountains in their own right steadily rise up to famous high Himalayan peaks like Everest, K2, and Annapurna, which you may have heard of before. Beyond those giants, only slightly lower in altitude, lies the cold plateau of Tibet.

What you find in the Himalayas depends on how high up you are and how much rain (or snow) the place receives. As you climb through the foothills, you'll pass through rhododendron forests and high Alpine pastures where yaks and goats graze, and cold, barren deserts in the "rain shadow" of the peaks. Going up still farther, you'll come to the bare rock and ice fields of the summits themselves.

The Andes mountain chain in South America is almost as high as the Himalayas, and many of the animals are similar.

Andes — viscacha, vicuña, spectacled bear.

Himalayas — marmot, chiru antelope, Himalayan black bear.

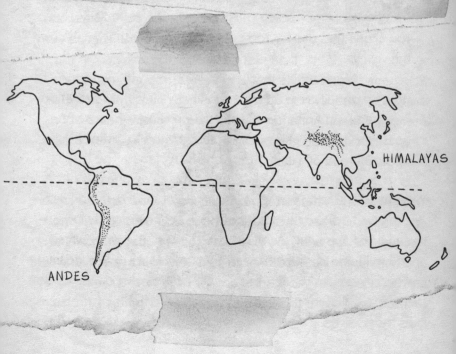

HIMALAYAS

ANDES

The time of year when you are traveling is the short season between the summer monsoon rains and the autumn, when the high passes become blocked with snow. When the sun is out it can feel like you're frying in the tropical heat, but as soon as a cloud passes or you enter the shade of a narrow ravine, you'll be struck by the sudden cold, especially when you cross the wild, icy torrents of meltwater that gush down the valleys.

High up on the sides of an enormous valley, the vegetation is low and wind-blasted. Small bushes cling to cracks and fissures in the rocks, hugging the ground to avoid being uprooted. The slope is steep, sheer in places. The trail you've been trudging all morning zigzags up and out of sight. At the head of the valley, peaks of bare rock and dazzling white snow rise up on either side. The slightly lower saddle-shaped gap in between is the Lohtang pass, which you will have to cross on your journey to get to the gleaming white pyramid of "Dangiroba," which pokes above the clouds in the far distance.

There is some movement on the trail ahead. Silhouetted against the sky, something huge and shaggy is approaching, lumbering slowly toward you. Your mind races through the possibilities.

What could it be?

A Himalayan brown bear — easily able to run you down?

A snow leopard — elusive and so well camouflaged that it's nearly invisible among the rocks and snows of its high mountain habitat?

A yeti — legendary hairy ape-man of the Himalayas, rumored to be dangerous?

SNOW LEOPARD

YETI

HIMALAYAN BROWN BEAR

The brown bear-leopard-yeti is getting closer. You can now make out two spindly human legs beneath the shambling mound. "Namaste," the woman says to you from beneath her heavy load of hay as she passes and continues back toward her village.

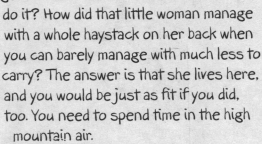

You continue up the path. With each step, you are forced to pause for breath. Your head feels dizzy and it feels as though iced water has been poured inside the veins of your legs.

How did you get so out of shape? It's the altitude. This high up, the air is so thin that you're struggling to take in enough oxygen with each breath. How do the locals do it? How did that little woman manage with a whole haystack on her back when you can barely manage with much less to carry? The answer is that she lives here, and you would be just as fit if you did, too. You need to spend time in the high mountain air.

You need to acclimatize. . . .

GETTING YOUR ACT TOGETHER
(Altitude: 2,000 meters)

Acclimatizing means getting your body used to living at a high altitude, where the air is thin and your body has to work harder to get the oxygen it needs. Red blood cells carry oxygen to your muscles to help them work. The air high in the mountains is at a lower pressure and so it's more spread out. When you spend time here your body makes more red blood cells to get around the problem. The result is that within a week or so you become acclimatized and no longer have difficulty walking, running, and doing exercise. Incidentally, if you then go down to sea level you feel super-fit for a while with all those extra red cells carrying the oxygen around. That's why many athletes like to train in places that are high above sea level.

You've decided to acclimatize at Darpeeling, a hill town where many years ago rich people used to come and have their holidays away from the stifling heat of the lowlands. Darpeeling is 2,000 meters above sea level with cool fresh air, blue skies, and a view in the distance of the snowy peak of "Dangiroba."

Darpeeling is the last town of any size where you can buy food, organize a guide, and perhaps hire some porters as well as a truck to take you to where the road ends in the Gali Kandaki Valley. It is here that you will organize your expedition.

There are several trekking agencies that equip would-be adventurers, and at one of these you meet up with Da-Lhamhu, a Sherpani (lady Sherpa), who is going to guide you on your trek as well as carry some of the gear. The Sherpas are a tribe of people who live in just a few valleys in the high Himalayas of Nepal. Over the years, they have earned a reputation for being the best guides and porters for Himalayan expeditions. More Sherpas than any other nationality have climbed Earth's highest peak, Mount Everest. Sherpa Tenzing Norgay was one of the first two men to get to the summit in 1953 (the other was Edmund Hillary, a New Zealander). Apa Sherpa climbed the mountain twelve times. Babu Chhiri Sherpa

bivouacked on the summit for twenty-one hours. He also set the record for the fastest ascent. Da-Lhamhu hasn't been on that many expeditions but, having been raised in the mountains, she should be able to assist you, translate the local language, and get your expedition equipped for the journey ahead.

Getting equipped

You're going to need equipment for all levels in the mountains. Firstly, you'll have to carry basic trekking equipment like sturdy boots, a tent, and cooking gear. Then, when you make your actual ascent of "Dangiroba," you'll need some highly specialized gear like crampons, ice axes, and oxygen tanks. All this climbing equipment will only be useful for your attempt at the summit. For the rest of your expedition, it will be useless deadweight that somebody will have to carry. To get to the remote monastery of Thamap, where the real climbing begins, you have a long and arduous journey ahead of you. You'll have to organize how you will transport all this equipment the entire way since there are no transportation-friendly roads where you're going.

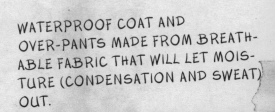

WATERPROOF COAT AND OVER-PANTS MADE FROM BREATHABLE FABRIC THAT WILL LET MOISTURE (CONDENSATION AND SWEAT) OUT.

This means you're going to need human porters or animals to carry it all. You can hire both at villages along the way, though they're not likely to want to travel beyond the next village, at which point you'll need to get more carriers.

- Light easy-to-dry clothing.
- Other useful items: A walking stick or trekking poles.
- Specialized mountain gear for you and Da-Lhamhu. That stuff will stay sealed in two knapsacks that are not to be opened until the real climbing starts (we'll look at it in more detail in chapter seven).

Da-Lhamhu says you can buy most of your food supplies here at Darpeeling. You'll also be able to buy more provisions at villages along your route, but you can't depend on that.

By the end of your shopping spree, you have eight sacks of lentils, rice, and other dry, easy-to-carry food, not to mention your knapsacks of mountain-climbing gear.

KNAPSACK

HIKING
BOOTS

TREKKING
POLE

About the author

Writer and broadcaster Simon Chapman is a self-confessed jungle addict, making expeditions whenever he can. His travels have taken him to tropical forests all over the world, from Borneo and Irian Jaya to the Amazon.

The story of his search for a mythical Giant Ape in the Bolivian rainforest, *The Monster of the Madidi*, was published in 2001. He has also had numerous articles and illustrations published in magazines in Great Britain and the United States, including *Wanderlust*, *BBC Wildlife*, and *South American Explorer*. He has written and recorded for BBC Radio 4, and has lectured on the organization of jungle expeditions at the Royal Geographical Society, of which he is a fellow. When not exploring, Simon lives with his wife and his two young children in Lancaster, England, where he teaches high school physics.